**Legend:**
- LIVING
- DESCENDANT
- DECEASED

**Sidebar labels (top to bottom):**
- ...OW OAK
- 12. HUNDRED HORSE CHESTNUT
- 13. PAWLING SYCAMORE
- 14. THE BIG TREE
- 15. LIBERTY TREE
- 16. HELEN KELLER WATER OAK
- 17. ANNE FRANK CHESTNUT TREE
- 18. GRAN ABUELO | 19. OLD TJIKKO
- 20. JURUPA OAK
- 21. PANDO

**28. Jaya Sri Maha Bodhi (Sri Lanka):** *This sacred fig tree supposedly grew from a sapling of the tree where the Buddha attained enlightenment. Millions of pilgrims visit it each year to pray and make offerings.*

**29. The Sisters (Lebanon):** *Folklore says that these trees were the source of the olive branch that Noah found at the end of the flood. Over the past 5,000 years, these olive trees have survived climate changes, disease, and civilization growth.*

**30. Gümeli Porsuğu (Turkey):** *This 4,100-year-old yew tree was named a Memorial Tree in 2018. It saw the surrounding area turn into a major coal production center in the 1800s.*

**31. Te Matua Ngahere (New Zealand):** *Te Matua Ngahere—which means "Father of the Forest" in Māori—is a remnant of an ancient rainforest. To protect this 1,500-year-old kauri tree from disease, Māori guardians require that visitors wash their footwear before and after visiting.*

**32. Abuelo Carob (Argentina):** *The 1,200-year-old tree was part of a carob forest that lasted until the railroads arrived in the 1850s. Pieces of old pottery suggest that aborigines lived alongside these trees long before the nearby town of Merlo was founded in 1755.*

**BUSHEL & PECK BOOKS**

Text copyright © 2023 by Ryan G. Van Cleave
Illustrations copyright © 2023 by Đốm Đốm

Published by Bushel & Peck Books, a family-run publishing house in
Fresno, California, that believes in uplifting children with the highest
standards of art, music, literature, and ideas. Find beautiful books for
gifted young minds at www.bushelandpeckbooks.com.

Type set in Bell MT, IM Fell English Pro, and Hurstmonceux
Some visuals sourced from Shutterstock.com: vintage tree frames
(Inkling Design), world map (juliawhite), vintage frames (yugoro),
tree rings (Karbo_Kreto)

Bushel & Peck Books is dedicated to fighting illiteracy all over the
world. For every book we sell, we donate one to a child in need—
book for book. To nominate a school or organization to receive free
books, please visit www.bushelandpeckbooks.com.

LCCN: 2022951185
ISBN: 9781638191254

First Edition

Printed in China

10 9 8 7 6 5 4 3 2 1

# THE
# WITNESS
# TREES

Ryan G. Van Cleave

Illustrated by Đóm Đóm

In the sweep of wind over grass,
near the pulse of rivers,
we stand,
monuments of bark
and age-curled green.

Our roots run deep—

they grip history,
a restless forever.

During an uprising in 1212,
King John of England held an
emergency session of Parliament
beneath this massive,
1,000-year-old tree in Sherwood
Forest. Afterward, it became
known as the Parliament Oak.

We bear witness
to the What,
When,
and How.

The Whos of the past
linger in the rings
and whorls of memory.

W e remember the heavy quiet
of Siddhartha as he calmed
his way to enlightenment.

*Siddhartha Gautama (circa
5th century BC)—the Buddha—
gained enlightenment after
meditating for seven days
beneath the Bodhi Tree.*

We remember the blackberry brambles
where light ambushed dark
like the onrush of dawn.

Major Oak, a 1,000-year-old oak
tree in Sherwood Forest, was the
rumored hideout of Robin Hood
(12th/13th century), the perhaps-
fictional folk hero who took from
the rich to give to the poor.

We remember the thump
atop Sir Isaac Newton's head
as an apple taught gravity.

*Sir Isaac Newton (1642-1726)*
*discovered gravity upon seeing an*
*apple fall from a Flower of Kent*
*apple tree in his garden.*

We remember the hushbomb
of happiness after chains surrendered
to the vocabulary of freedom.

In 1792, the Cotton Tree became the historic
symbol of Freetown, Sierra Leone, when
former African American slaves gained
their freedom by battling British soldiers.

This honey locust witnessed three deadly days of fighting (the Battle of Gettysburg) that was the turning point of the American Civil War. It also heard Abraham Lincoln deliver his famous 1863 speech to dedicate the Gettysburg National Cemetery.

Shut your eyes and listen.
In leafspeak and barksong,
our stories thrum
with stars, moon, and sun.

W e are the English oaks
handed to Jesse Owens
to the world-shaking
echo of applause.

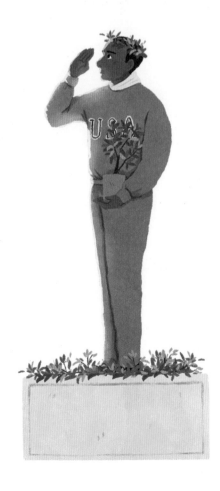

*In the 1936 Berlin Olympics, Jesse Owens (1913–1980)
became the first American track-and-field athlete
to win four gold medals. All winners received oak
saplings along with their medals, but German dictator
Adolf Hitler refused to shake the hand of a Black
man. Owens planted one sapling at Rhodes High
School in Cleveland, Ohio, where he trained. What
happened to the other three saplings is unknown.*

We are the hackberry,
gingko, and black pines
that swallowed the heatflash
of a thousand suns.

*Almost 170 trees somehow
survived the atomic bomb blast
in Hiroshima, Japan, on August
6, 1945. They are collectively
called* hibaku jumoku—*the
survivor trees.*

We are the redwood called Luna
that cradled a woman
who braved wind, cold,
and the roar of chainsaw.

*In 1997, Julia Butterfly Hill
(b. 1974) climbed a 180-foot,
1,500-year-old California redwood
to protest the logging of old-
growth forests. She stayed in
Luna—the name she gave the tree—
for 738 days before an agreement
was reached to protect Luna.*

We are the Callery pear tree
beneath the thunder-smash
of steel and fiery smoke
as two towers tumbled.

*Weeks after the World Trade
Center fell on September 11,
2001, recovery workers discovered
a Callery pear tree—crushed and
scorched, but miraculously still
alive. This tree became known as
the Survivor Tree.*

Through pearly dusk
and the orange-red of harvests.

*Located at Oxon Hill
Farm in Maryland,
this willow oak survived
the War of 1812 and
witnessed British soldiers
burning the White House,
the Capitol, and other
Washington DC buildings.*

Through lightning storms
and the moaning low
of wolves.

Legend has it that when
a queen and her hundred
knights got caught in a
ferocious storm, they
took shelter beneath
this huge tree. Whether
that's true or not, the
Hundred Horse Chestnut
is the largest and oldest
chestnut tree in the
world—it's estimated to
be 2,000 to 4,000 years
old. Even more surprising
is that it lives on the
side of Mount Etna, an
active volcano in Sicily!

Through wind-chime icicles
and long troughs of stillness.

*Known as the Pawling Sycamore, this sprawling tree saw George Washington and 12,000 Continental soldiers endure the brutal 1777 winter in Valley Forge. While no battle was fought here during that time, almost 2,000 people still died due to hunger, cold, and disease.*

Through the wet kiss
of a thousand-year-old squall.

The slow stampede of time
has laid its claim, yet . . .

The Big Tree of Rockport, Texas, is
one of the largest live oak trees in the
United States. It recently withstood
the devastation of Hurricane Harvey,
a Category 4 hurricane, but in its
1,000-year-plus lifetime, it survived
dozens of other hurricanes as well
as floods, droughts, and wildfires. It
even lived through artillery attacks
during the American Civil War!

We never forget the heft of lanterns
as liberty breathed life
beneath the canopy of night.

*In 1765, angry colonists filled the*
*branches of an elm tree with lanterns,*
*banners, and effigies against the British*
*soldiers' oppression. That elm became*
*known as the Liberty Tree. It was felled*
*in August 1775 by Loyalist troops.*

We never forget the firm fingers
of a radiant girl who clambered skyward
to cloudwhite and beyond.

*In her autobiography, Helen Keller (1880-1968)—who was deaf and blind—recounted how her childhood teacher, Anne Sullivan, rescued her from a beloved water oak tree when a fast-moving storm blew in. A tornado claimed the tree in 2015.*

We never forget shadow-silent Anne,
that caged bird who fluttered
branch to branch in dewy dreams.

In soil and shale
or the caverndeep
of memory,
we remain.

Then and Now,
Tomorrow and Always,
we continue.

*Anne Frank (1929-1945) is a well-known
Jewish Holocaust victim because of her
memoir,* The Diary of a Young Girl. *For
two years, she only saw the world—and
a horse chestnut tree—through an attic
window that was usually covered with
blackout curtains so her family could
stay hidden from the Nazi soldiers.
The tree was cut down in 2010 after
suffering severe storm damage.*

# We are Gran Abuelo.

Gran Abuelo is a
3,600-year-old Patagonian
cypress in Chile.

# We are Old Tjikko.

Old Tjikko is a
9,550-year-old Norway
spruce on Fulujället
Mountain in Sweden.

We are the
Jurupa Oak.

The Jurupa Oak is a
13,000-year-old Palmer's
oak in the Jurupa
Mountains in California.

We are Pando.

Pando is a colony of quaking aspens in
Utah's Fishlake National Forest that
could be 80,000 years old. Although
it's made up of more than 40,000
stems, it's a single organism since it's
all connected by a vast underground
root system.

Above, an avalanche of stars.
Below, the ocean of earth.

Within, the uncounted lives
birthed, bloomed, and plucked
from the gardens we tend.

We endure.

We remember.

We witness.

# ALL ABOUT WITNESS TREES

## AUTHOR'S NOTE

When I was ten, my father took me to California to seek out a hidden 4,800-year-old Great Basin bristlecone pine called Methuselah. We searched but didn't find it, though we did see plenty of towering redwoods in Hendy Woods State Park—some of them were 2,000 years old. Ancient, but not by Methuselah's standards!

Still, I never forgot the sense of history embedded within their gnarled trunks. Those trees were tangible historical memory. Even at my young age, I felt their awesome power.

For many people, trees have become the roses they don't stop to smell. We allow them to hide in plain sight. But trees are the oldest organisms on Earth—they are a vital, lasting connection to our past.

## WHAT IS A WITNESS TREE?

While any truly old tree has witnessed many things, Witness Trees get their name from being present for key moments

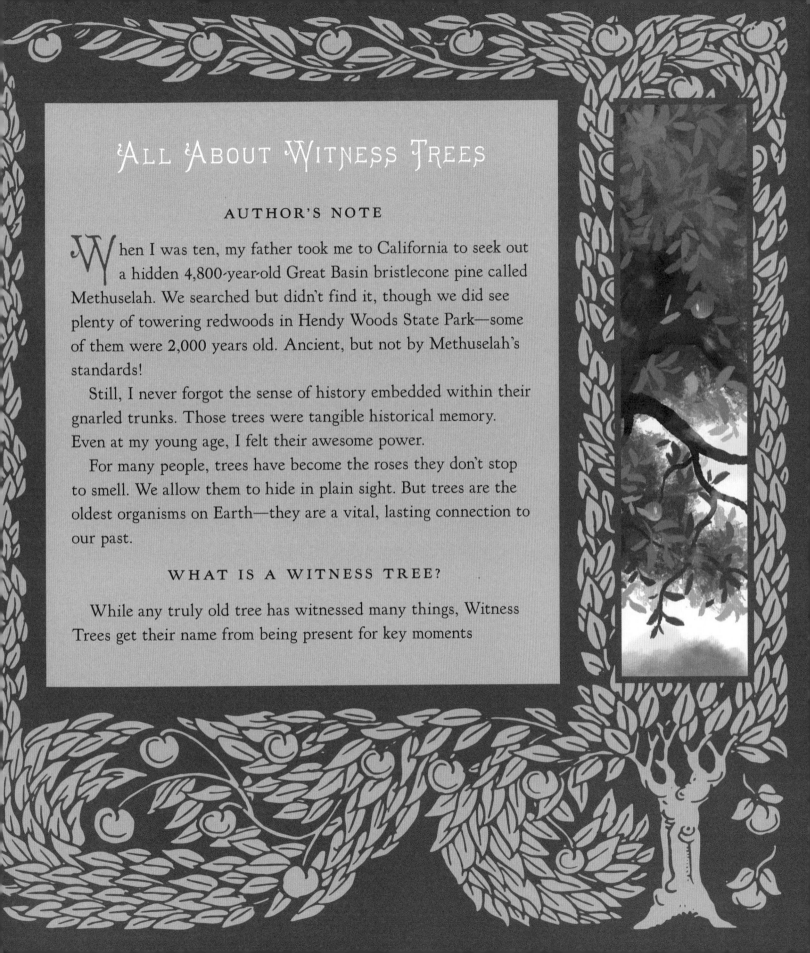

in history, which means they've borne witness to many of humanity's greatest triumphs and struggles. Many have bullets covered over by new layers of bark and wood, or carry visible scars that often never fade.

## AN UNCERTAIN FUTURE

What's disheartening is that some of the most ancient, important trees are now gone.

- In 1964, a graduate student got permission to take a core sample from Prometheus, a 4,900-year-old Great Basin bristlecone pine in Nevada. Somehow, the entire tree got cut down instead.
- The Senator, a 3,500-year-old Pond cypress in Florida, burned to ash in 2012 when a woman started a fire inside the hollow of the tree to keep herself warm.
- Helen Keller's water oak tree was so damaged by insects and a tornado that it was taken down in 2015.

The exact number of Witness Trees in the world is unknown— it's difficult to date trees without damaging them, so some Witness Trees are only recognized as such once they've died.

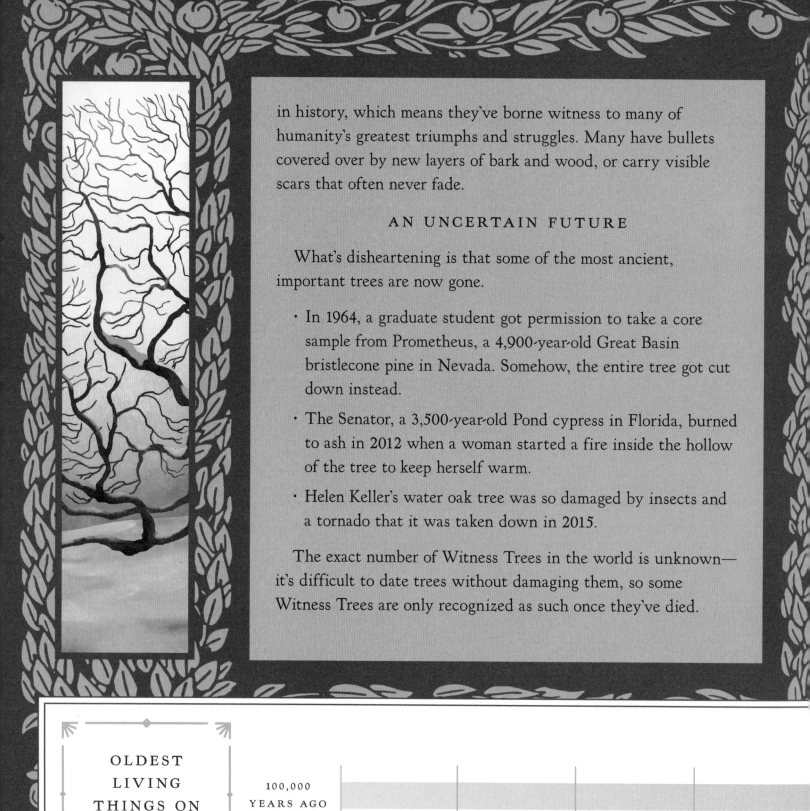

OLDEST
LIVING
THINGS ON
EARTH

100,000
YEARS AGO

*80,000 years: Pando*
*(quaking aspen)*